VOGUE GUIDE TO Patchwork & Quilting

STEIN AND DAY *Publishers* NEW YORK
IN ASSOCIATION WITH THE CONDÉ NAST PUBLICATIONS LTD

First published in the United States of America
by Stein and Day *Publishers* in 1974
in association with The Condé Nast Publications Ltd
Copyright © 1973 The Condé Nast Publications Ltd

Library of Congress Catalog Card No. 73–92190

Printed in Great Britain. Collins Clear-Type Press

Stein and Day *Publishers* Scarborough House, Briarcliff Manor, N.Y. 10510

SBN 0–8128–1686–2

Editor: Judy Brittain
Technical Editors: Ian Alexander and
Susan Whitehead
Editor Condé Nast Books: Alex Kroll

Acknowledgements:
Drawings: Susan Whitehead.
Photographers: Karl Stoecker –
Front Cover and pages 34, 36,
37, 40, 60, 62, 63, 64. Horst –
pages 4 and end papers. John
Swannell – pages 12, 23, 25, 68.
Derek Butler – pages 38, 39, 41,
42, 43, 44, 69. John Wingrove –
back cover and pages 45, 78, 79.
Denis Short – 46. Victoria and
Albert Museum – pages 70–75.
Blaise Castle House Museum –
pages 76–77. John Minshall –
page 80.

Contents

Introduction

Patchwork is essentially a mosaic of fabric pieces seamed edge to edge. Quilting, from the Latin *culcita* meaning a cushion, is defined as a coverlet or garment of padding, held between two layers of fabric by crossed rows of sewing. The natural outcome of these two crafts is, of course, patchwork quilts. However, we have dealt with each of these crafts separately in order to make it clear to the reader that there are many ways of using both patchwork and quilting beyond making bedspreads.

Patchwork has been carried out in America since pioneer times, although it was not really fashionable until the end of the eighteenth century when silks and printed cottons became cheap and common enough to cut up whilst still having some wear left in them.

Most households owned a quilt, plain on one side and patchwork on the other. A patchwork quilt was an essential part of a bride's dowry; not only were old scraps of fabric used, but pieces with sentimental value such as the bride's first party dress, or scraps of her mother's wedding dress, or even baby clothes were worked into the design. Very often the paper patterns cut from the template were made from the bride's old love letters. In this way family history can be worked into a patchwork even today.

Although people may not have scrap bags from which to make patchwork, there are now many beautiful fabrics on the market to choose from; this means that a modern patchwork can be designed from start to finish, and the fabric specially bought.

Most of the patchwork examples in this book have been made up in this way, but individual interpretations of the same idea are always possible. Patchwork technique is very simple; it is really the choice of fabric and the way it is put together that makes a lovely article.

Quilting is a traditional craft, going back, in the British Isles, to the thirteenth century. As a cottage industry it was carried on in South Wales and the North of England, and was still flourishing at the beginning of this century.

Quilted bed furniture of all kinds, petticoats, doublets, and breeches were fashionable in the seventeenth and eighteenth centuries, and today quilting is once again in demand for clothes such as jackets and waistcoats, and cord quilting when used, for example, for decorative motifs and monograms.

Quilting can also be done by machine which, of course, makes the whole thing very much easier than in the old days when every stitch of huge bedspreads was worked by hand.

This book gives many ideas for both patchwork and quilting: we hope that when you have studied it, you will find that you are inspired with many more ideas of your own.

Mrs Wyatt Emory Cooper – Gloria Vanderbilt, the painter, photographed in her beautiful all patchwork bedroom. The mosaic effect of all the various textures and shapes used together from floor to ceiling shows how patchwork can be really dazzling for interior decoration.

Patchwork

How to start

Fabrics
Small scraps of fabric can be used for patchwork, especially for early samples when you may not wish to attempt anything elaborate.

Some materials are much easier to handle than others. Cotton is a good fabric to begin with since it does exactly what you want it to; it also makes crisp sharp folds and is easy to sew. Hessian and other loosely woven fabrics should be avoided since they fray badly and cannot be worked into neat geometric shapes.

Use fabrics of the same texture and strength in a piece of work; for instance, try not to combine cotton and silk, since they will present wash and care problems later.

Paper
You will need large sheets of strong paper, a good quality cartridge paper, or very old letters, stiff envelopes, and bills can also be cut up (see Introduction); each patchwork shape needs its own paper pattern.

Needles, thread etc
Use the right kind of thread for the material, eg a silk thread for silk fabric. This also applies to needles; a fine needle is best for silk and a slightly thicker needle for cotton.

Dressmakers' pins are useful, and a roll of sticky tape to keep the fabric round the paper pattern till all the pieces have been sewn together.

You will need a pencil, paper scissors, and a craft knife for cutting round templates and patterns.

For planning your patchwork from the very start you will need to get isometric graph paper which is available at most office stationers and craft stores.

Templates

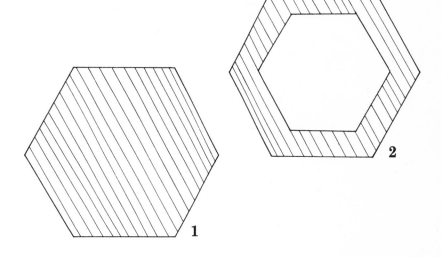

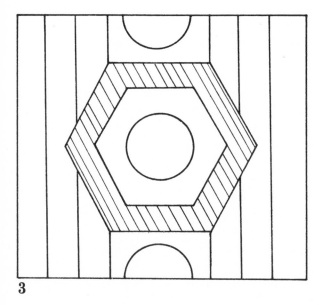

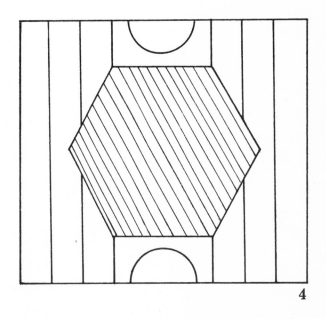

A template is the 'master-copy' of the shape to be used in a piece of work. It can be made from metal or strong card.

You will need a solid template for cutting out the actual shapes (fig. 1), and a window template, the same size and shape but with the middle cut out (fig. 2), which is used for placing over patterned fabric (fig. 3) to find

the best parts of the pattern to cut out with the solid template (fig. 4).

Although metal templates can be bought from good needlecraft stores, it can be more interesting, once you feel sufficiently confident, to make your own templates from stiff card. The only disadvantage is that these do wear out and eventually need replacing.

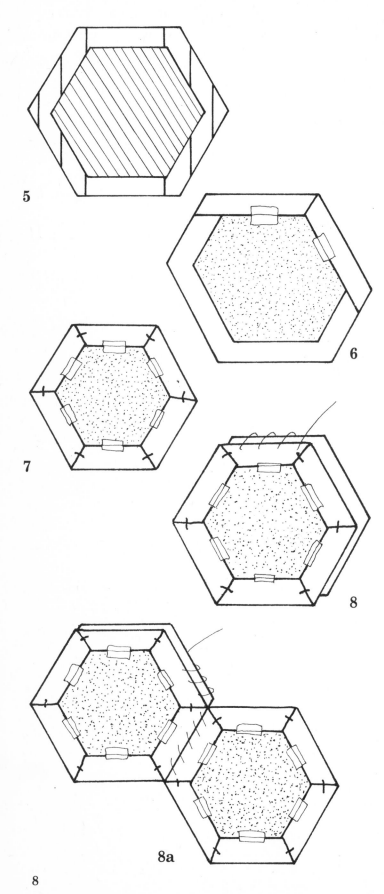

5

6

7

8

8a

The hexagon

This is the traditional shape in patchwork (fig. 1); it is most commonly used in the 'star' motif, a group made up of one central hexagon surrounded by six others. The hexagon 'star' is a good shape to try out first, since it can be enlarged to make things like place mats or an entire object such as a bedspread can be made up of these shapes scattered over a plain fabric. Having decided to make a hexagon 'star', begin by cutting out seven paper patterns with a hexagon template. Then place the window template over the chosen fabric, selecting the areas of pattern which will look best; now place the paper patterns on the fabric. Allowing just over $\frac{1}{4}''$ all round the fabric, cut out your hexagon shapes (fig. 5).

It is important to remember at this stage to cut out all the patches so that the straight grain of the fabric runs in the same direction in each case. This will prevent the work from 'bubbling' when all the paper patterns have been removed at the end.

Once all the fabric shapes have been cut, fold the material over the paper pattern, one side at a time, and secure with a piece of sticky tape (fig. 6).

It may help with a slippery fabric to put a small stitch in each corner (fig. 7). Two shapes are then placed right sides together, and one edge is sewn with a small hemming stitch (fig. 8).

Of course, once more than two shapes are involved, they cannot be folded completely flat, just enough to make a neatly sewn edge possible (fig. 8a).

To get straight edges, join single hexagons down sides and then mount the whole patchwork onto border material. If border fabric is not being used then simply join on the single hexagons down sides, cut them in half, and hem. When the required number of shapes have been sewn together, the paper patterns can be removed, and the patchwork pressed lightly (fig. 9 back view, fig. 10 front).

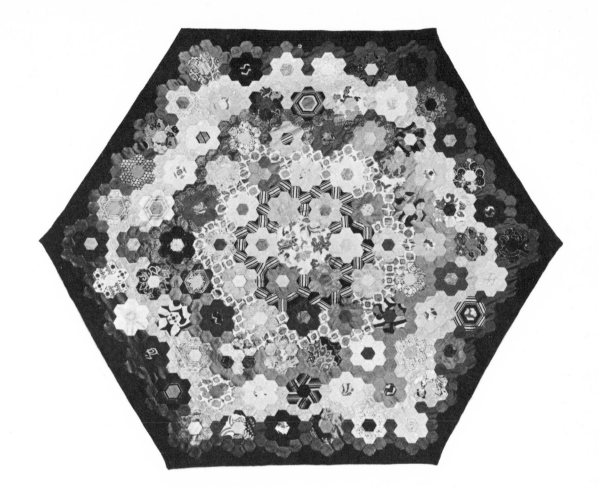

A rich and beautiful hexagon table cloth
designed by Mrs Joanna Vignola illustrates
the wonderful effects which can be achieved by
clever use of the hexagon and choice of fabrics.
The whole effect is amplified by mounting the
design on a hexagon shaped border

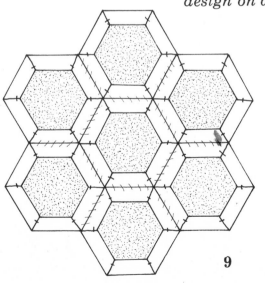

9

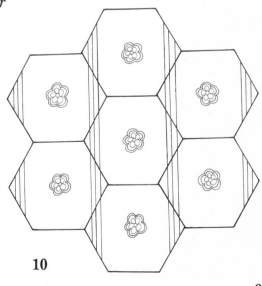

10

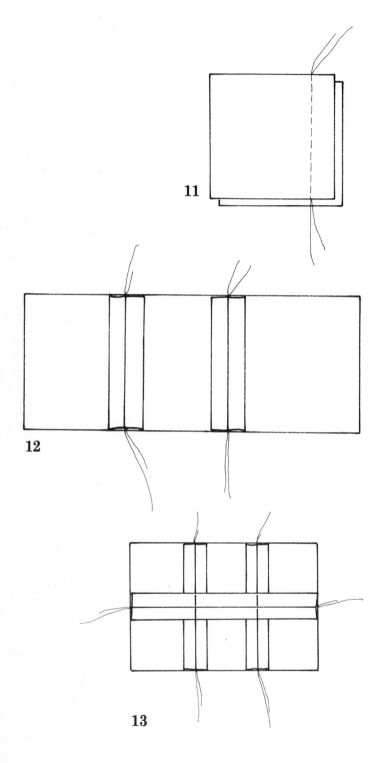

11

12

13

Machining

Patchwork is nearly always done by hand, because of the small, complicated shapes involved; however, very large simple shapes, such as squares, can be machined.

This can be achieved by using the presser foot of the machine and ordinary running stitch (fig. 11). You do not need to make paper patterns, or use a template, but the same care has to be taken in making sure that the straight grain of the fabric runs the same way in all the pieces.

First machine two pieces together (fig. 11). Then make long strips, pressing the seams open (fig. 12).

Once the long strips are sewn together in the same way, patchwork emerges (figs. 13 and 13a).

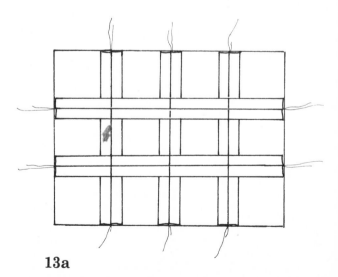

13a

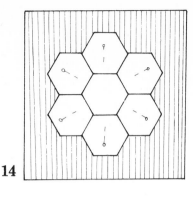

14

Lining & interlining

Hexagon 'stars' or other motifs can be lined individually, for instance if they are to be used as place mats. Pin the motif onto the backing fabric so that the right side of the patchwork is uppermost (fig. 14). Cut round it, allowing $\frac{1}{2}''$ all round (fig. 15). Clip the inside corners (fig. 16). Turn in the raw edges completely, and hem neatly (fig. 17).

A large object, such as a cot cover, may need a synthetic interlining for extra warmth, as well as a plain lining. The interlining should be basted to the patchwork at evenly spaced intervals (fig. 18). The lining can then be sewn to the patchwork, right sides together, with one end left free (fig. 19).

Turn right sides out, finishing remaining edge neatly with hemming stitch (fig. 20).

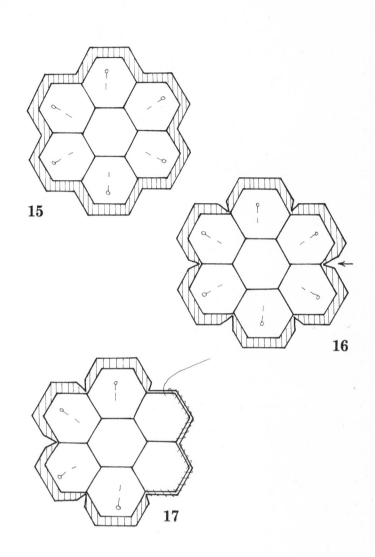

15

16

17

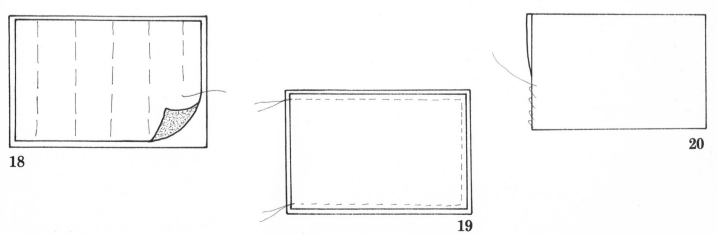

18

19

20

Embroidery and patchwork

Once the patchwork article is finished and the sticky tape and paper patterns removed, simple embroidery stitches can be added to produce some interesting effects. For example, use feather stitch round the center hexagon of a 'star' motif (fig. 21), or an initial or even the name of the patchwork maker in french knots in the center of the shape (fig. 22). A group of children could each make a 'star' motif and put their own names in each center; in this way the finished patchwork would have memento value in years to come. Small flowers in lazy daisy stitch round a central hexagon in plain fabric also add interest (fig. 23).

The same ideas can be carried out with machined shapes. Machine zig-zag can be used down the seams of machined patchwork in a decorative way (fig. 24).

Crazy Patchwork is a form of patchwork which needs no templates and no regular shapes. You simply join pieces of fabric together like crazy paving stones and finish with feather stitch embroidery. The photograph shows a beautiful example of crazy patchwork designed by Mrs Naomi Langley

21

22

23

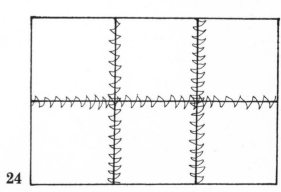

24

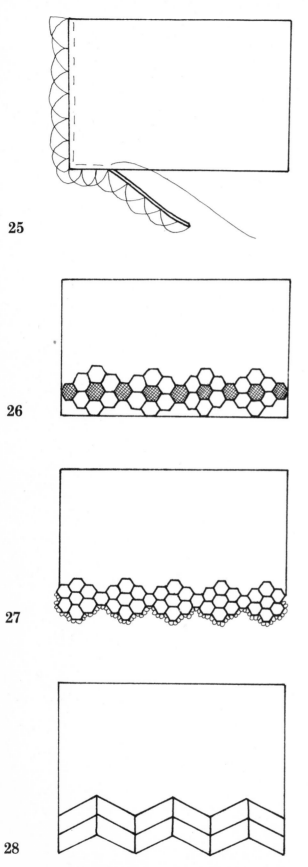

25

26

27

28

Borders and trimmings

Patchwork objects such as cushions and bedspreads may need extra finishing in the making-up process.

For example, a lace or braid trimming can be tacked under the edge of the patchwork before the lining is attached (fig. 25). If you have made up a great many motifs, perhaps as samples, then they can be sewn along the edge of a bedspread (fig. 26), and used in conjunction with a lace edging (fig. 27), or used by themselves to make an ornate edging (fig. 28).

Appliqué and patchwork

Appliqué is a variation of patchwork; it is the technique of applying 'cut-outs' to a background, as opposed to joining one cut-out to another. It can be carried out by hand or by using a machine.

If you make up a simple patchwork object, such as one composed of squares, a more complicated effect can be produced by applying further shapes to the finished article, especially small curved shapes such as a feather pattern, not suitable for sewing edge to edge (fig. 29).

The edges are difficult to turn in on these small shapes, so it is easier to use a suitable edging stitch, such as herringbone or blanket stitch (fig. 30).

Use fabrics that will handle easily, and remember to match like fabrics (cottons with cottons, silks with silks etc).

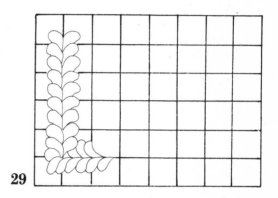

29

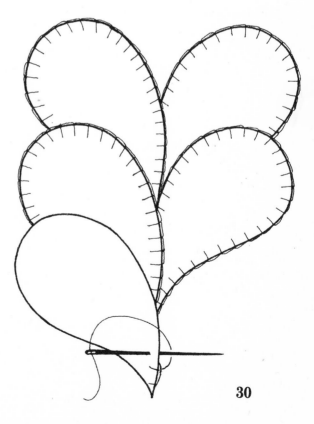

30

31

Different shapes for patchwork

All the shapes in the following pages can be made up into individual motifs or sewn onto larger articles such as cushions. This may be useful in helping to acquire a 'feel' for the work. Some of the combinations of shapes are quite complicated, but once you have tried them you will have enough experience to attempt a really large patchwork.

The rectangle (fig. 31)
This is a useful shape for both machine and hand work; it can be used with the square to make up large areas quickly (fig. 32).

The triangle (fig. 33)
This can be made up horizontally with other triangles (fig. 34), as a star (fig. 35), or as the familiar hexagon (fig. 36).

The diamond (fig. 37)
This is a good shape to use on its own with a variety of contrasting fabrics (fig. 38), or with a combination of triangles and diamonds (fig. 39).

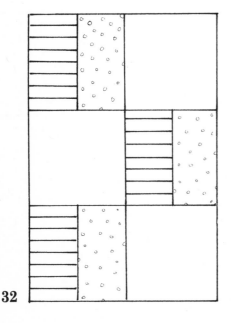

32

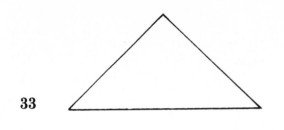

33

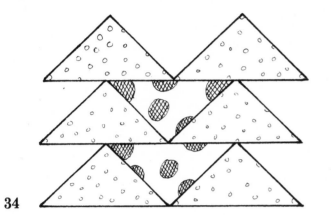

34

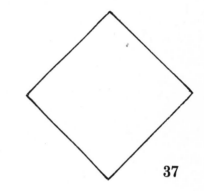

37

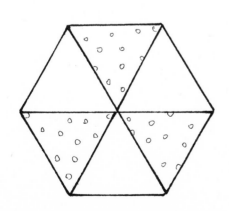

35

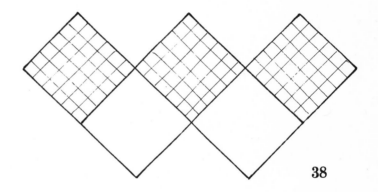

38

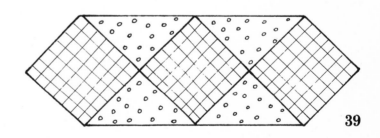

39

Different shapes for patchwork

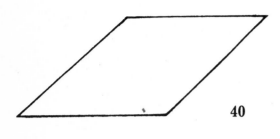

40

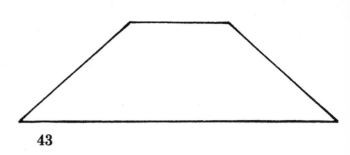

43

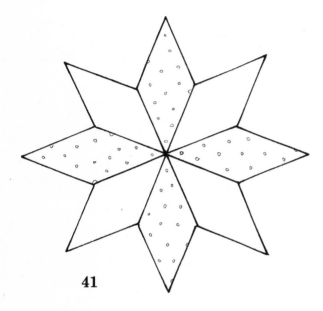

41

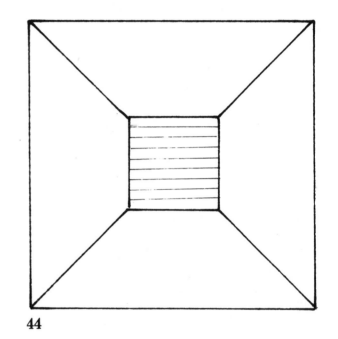

44

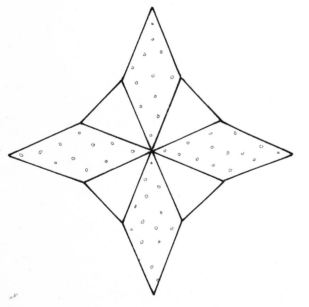

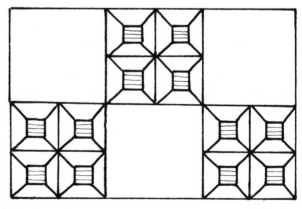

45

18

The rhomboids

Rhomboid A (fig. 40) can be the most adaptable shape of all; used with itself alone it forms a star (fig. 41), and in conjunction with triangles it makes a beautiful variation on the 'star' motif (fig. 42).

Rhomboid B (fig. 43) is another adaptable shape. It can be used with a central square (fig. 44), and because of its simple outline it can be machined as well as handsewn. It becomes interesting and intricate when used with large and small squares (fig. 45).

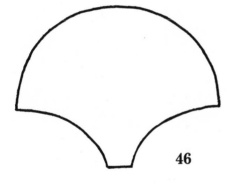

46

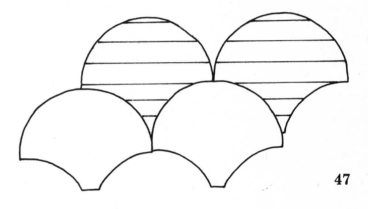

47

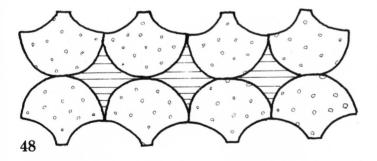

48

The shell

The traditional shell pattern (fig. 46) is often found in quilting. It is best used on its own, made up from plain and patterned fabrics (fig. 47). The template is a little more difficult to make and the shapes do need skill in making up, but these, reversed and applied to a plain fabric, can make an interesting scalloped edging (fig. 48).

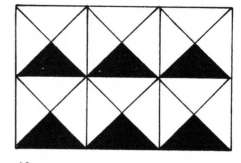

49

Optical effects

By using contrasting tones and very simple shapes it is quite easy to achieve some extraordinary optical illusions. Using the triangle with light and dark fabrics (fig. 49) you can get an illusion of depth; and by changing the layout of the triangles, but still using dark and light fabrics, you get a fractured effect (fig. 50). Using the diamond and two rhomboid 'A's' with contrasting fabrics gives a three dimensional pattern (fig. 51).

50

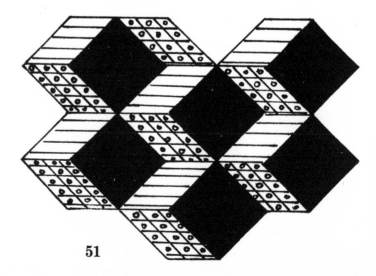

51

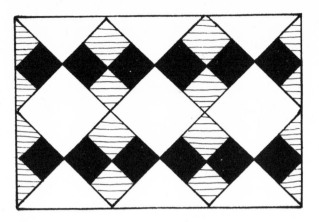

52

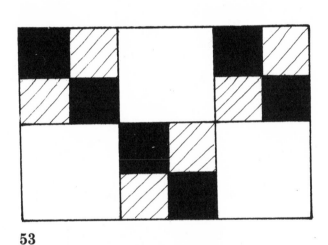

53

Shapes in different sizes

Large and small shapes used together can break up big areas of patchwork and make them look quite complicated. The three shapes illustrated are particularly good for machine patchwork, where intricate shapes cannot be used, and shapes of the same size can become monotonous. Fig. 52 shows the diamond pattern, fig. 53 shows squares, and fig. 54, rectangles.

54

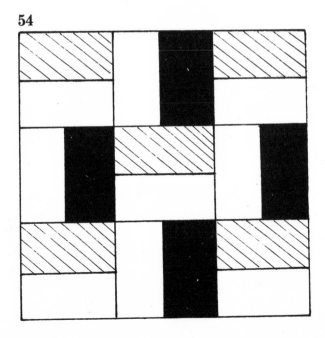

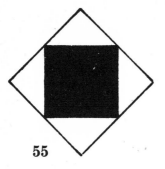

55

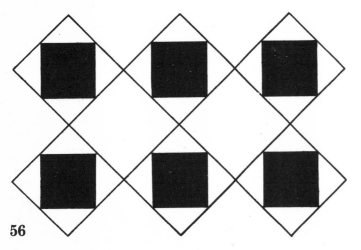

56

Different shapes used together

You can begin to achieve quite a complicated build-up of ideas by just using a combination of two different shapes and sizes. For example, four triangles and a square, made into a square (fig. 55). This can then be used with squares of the same size (fig. 56).

Variations can be achieved by using dark and light fabrics (fig. 57).

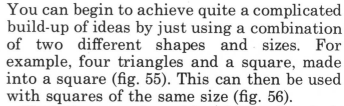

57

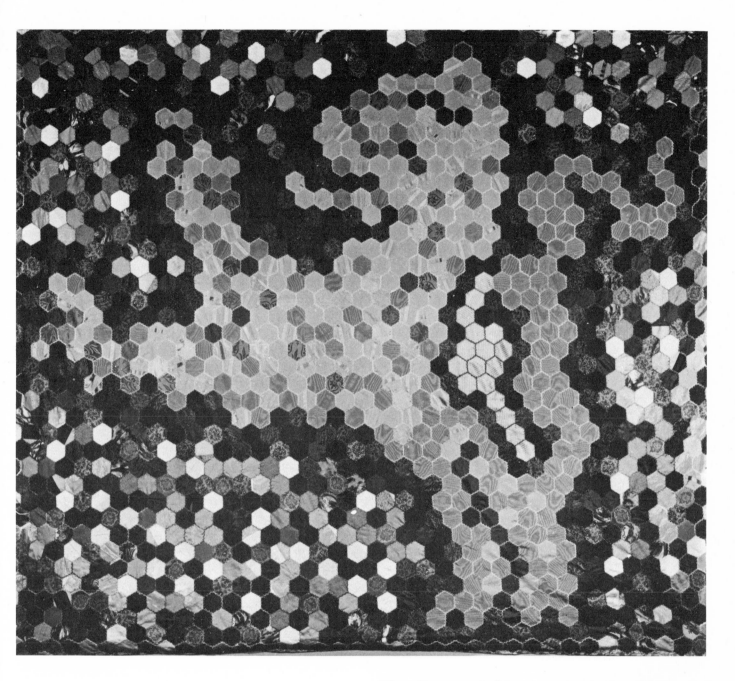

The Rampant Lion crest of the Bishop of Dover was incorporated into a bedspread for him designed by Mrs R Petty. This is a beautiful example of the use of light and dark shades to give a pictorial effect

Plain and patterned fabrics

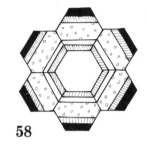

58

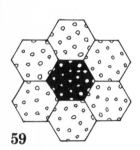

59

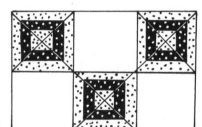

60

Using the simplest patchwork shapes and plain and patterned fabrics together, you can get some really fascinating effects. For example, use the hexagon 'star' motif with plain fabric in the center and striped fabric bordering it (fig. 58); or simply use a patterned fabric for the center with a plain fabric border (fig. 59), or use striped fabrics for triangles, formed into a square with plain fabric, perhaps in different colors, for squares of the same size (fig. 60).

A centerpiece for a bedspread or cushion is made by using varying sizes of rhomboid A in many different fabrics, put together to form a star (fig. 61).

61

Simply by using plain and patterned fabrics and one shape, very beautiful designs can be achieved. This star bedspread is designed by Mrs Naomi Langley who has used plain fabrics to outline her overall patterns in this marvelously worked out design

Expanding ideas and designs

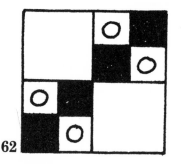

62

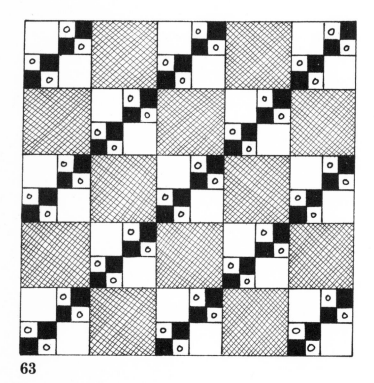

63

If you become really inspired by patchwork and want to work on a large scale for bedspreads, wall-hangings, curtains etc, then try making up one motif, or small area, and repeat the design in a variety of ways (fig. 62).

In this way you can build up a striped pattern (fig. 63), a zig-zag (fig. 64), chevrons (fig. 65) and squares (fig. 66). None of the shapes need be small or complicated, and if you work on a really large scale then the patchwork can be machined.

Once you begin thinking about patchwork you will find that ideas come flooding in from all over the place, even from such mundane things as man-hole covers, brickwork – anything, in fact, which is made up in simple geometric shapes. Tile floors can be a ceaseless inspiration.

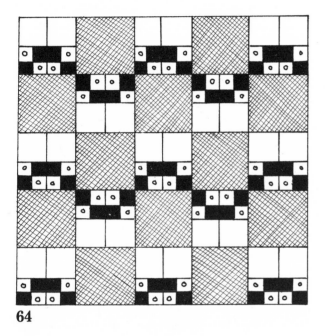

64

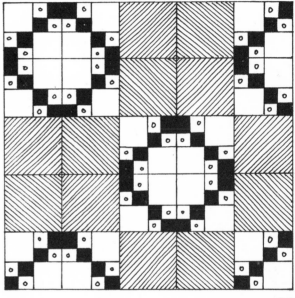

66

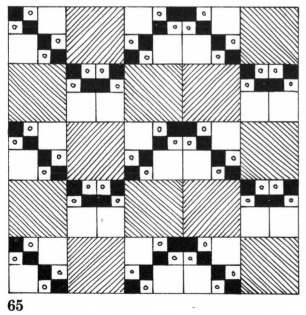

65

Expanding ideas and designs

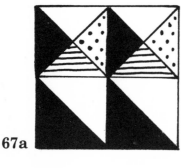

67a

By repeating small triangles in four different fabrics, and big triangles in two different fabrics (fig. 67a), you can get an interesting effect of broken lines and patterns. This pattern combination can be used in bigger pattern shapes (fig. 67b), and by joining four of these together you will get further patterns forming within the existing shapes.

A very simple shape like the triangle used with fabrics toning down from dark to light with prints such as dots ranging from large to small (fig. 68), will give some marvelous optical designs.

67b

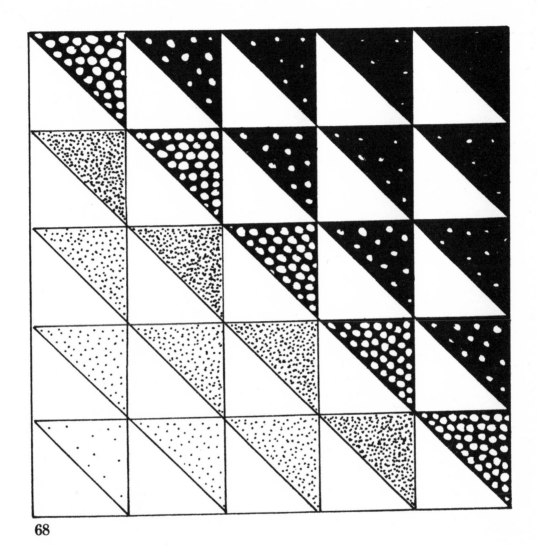

68

Expanding ideas and designs

Rhomboids, diamonds, and triangles used together with striped and flowered or dotted fabrics (fig. 69) give a regular trellis pattern, with the stripes diminishing into plain fabrics to give a striking tonal effect.

Appliqué patchwork on a simple square motif patchwork will give some very interesting and amusing results. With machined squares of three different fabrics apply a box shape in a fourth fabric with the lid and inside of the box in the same fabrics as the main patchwork (fig. 70). This gives a very intricate look to something which is, in fact, extremely simple and easy to do.

69

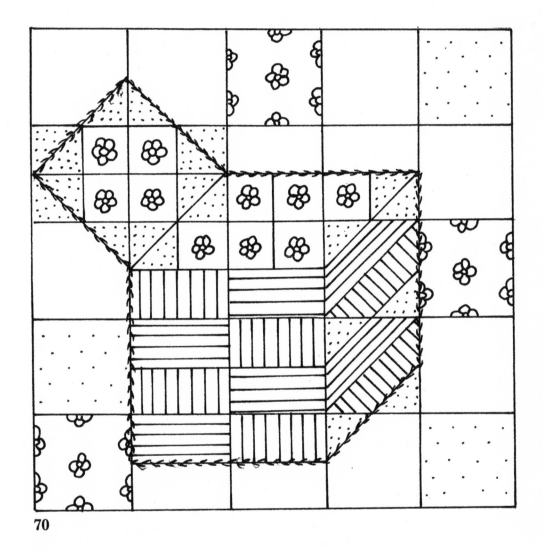

70

Working with color

Having dealt with the shapes, patterns, fabrics, and toning of patchwork we now come to color and the use of this for patchwork.

If you are designing your own patchwork from the very start and have a special color scheme in mind, remember that the main color of the scheme can become the background fabric. It can also be used in large template shapes or even as a surface for smaller, more intricate patchwork application. The front cover shawl and the back cover bedspread demonstrate this use of background color.

Amazingly exotic rooms have been designed with patchwork, as the inside cover illustrations demonstrate. At the front of this book the left hand picture shows a bedroom in which the patchwork walls and ceiling have been kept harmonious by the use of a white background even though the patterns and subsidiary colors vary. The bedspread, cushions, and floor are also kept harmonious by the use of mutual rust reds and tawny yellows. On the right is an Old America patchwork quilt made in the 1870's by the pioneering women of that time. This is a very simple design with the basic shapes worked into large squares, which in turn are joined by a background of soft yellow. Both these bedspreads are deeply bordered with contrasting paisley fabrics. The quilted patchwork wall-hanging above the Old America quilt is called 'Barn Raising', and was made at approximately the same time. It depicts harvesting in symbolic pictures set into squares, and illustrates very well how effective the use of only 4 colors can be.

The illustrations inside the back cover show on the left hand page a living room with a made to measure sofa covering in quilted patchwork. The different shaped stars stand out dramatically from the black and white ground. The startling effect is increased by making some of the stars black and white too. Cushions of the same patterning are added and the whole concept echoes the flower medallion flooring. On the right, in the foreground, a simple nine patch and square design covers a floor cushion, the large blue squares contrasting with the nine patches. The table, hung with a 'Straight Furrows' design echoes the pinky reds of the mural and picks up the yellows of the floor cushions. The other floor cushions in really simple squares and triangles show that even with a limited range of fabric and color a very decorative design can be achieved.

The use of color can be restricted or brilliantly varied as long as there is a theme going through to bind the design or designs together.

For further patchwork ideas and designs a visit to the American Museum in Britain, at Claverton Manor, Bath, is recommended. This museum houses a very fine collection of American work.

Giant squares border this bedspread which is made up in triangles, strips and squares which get bigger and bigger as they work outwards. The small central shapes are delicately colored, and as they grow the color deepens

Front cover shawl

MATERIALS
Frilled shawl pattern in plain and printed lawn.

¼ yard each of 8 different prints, 4 light and 4 dark colored. 2 yards of plain background fabric, and 2 yards of check fabric for lining, frill, and circles.

HOW TO MAKE
Cut out templates from illustrations. Cut 20 squares 6½″×6½″ (this allows for ¼″ seam turnings) plus five squares cut to make 10 triangles, all in background fabric. Cut fan shapes (you will need 102), allowing an extra ¼″ at the quarter circle end. Cut 20 quarter circles.

Sew six of the fan sections together using alternate dark and light prints. You can use machine zig-zag stitch, or sew together by hand and embroider later. Position fan on square, and stitch or zig-zag round side of lower edges. Place quarter circle in position overlapping curved edge ¼″ over fan. Stitch or zig-zag all round. Cut away fabric from behind. Join squares as illustrated. Attach frill and lining.

This fan motif can be continued for larger surfaces such as floor cushions and bedspreads.

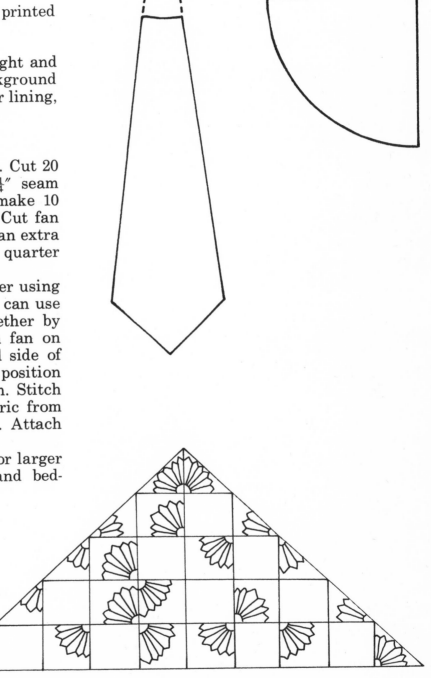

Pinafore dress

MATERIALS
Full-length jumper pattern.

Size 8 takes 3 yards furnishing fabric, and 1 yard fruit motif furnishing fabric. Any definite motif fabric can be used for the bodice and hem appliqué. 1 yard muslin.

HOW TO MAKE
Make one circular template of $2\frac{3}{4}''$ diameter and another of $2''$ diameter, and from these cut 41 $2''$ circles and four $2\frac{3}{4}''$ circles using fruit motifs as centers of each circle. Cut muslin out to bodice pattern and mount circles as photograph. Join circles together with close zig-zag stitch, and zig-zag completely round each circle. When all circles are mounted and joined, cut away muslin between circles. Cut out and make the skirt in the usual way. Join bodice to skirt. Cut further motifs of fruit pattern, and apply to hem of skirt by hand.

Wrapover skirt

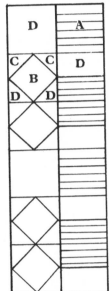

MATERIALS
Wrapover skirt pattern.

Size 8 takes 5 yards of main fabric. $\frac{1}{2}$ yard each of contrast B and C fabric, 1 yard of contrast D fabric. Shown here in household fabrics. Front panel of skirt is machine patchwork.

HOW TO MAKE
Make up seven strips in alternating panel designs. Panel 1 is composed of two 7″ squares, four 4″ squares and 16 3½″ sided triangles. Panel 2 is composed of four 7″ squares and four 2″ × 7″ rectangles. Use fabrics to contrast as shown on diagram. The finished area of these seven strips will measure approximately 40″ in length, 30″ in width. When completed, pin front panel paper pattern to patchwork, and cut out. Make rest of skirt in the usual way.

Striped bolster

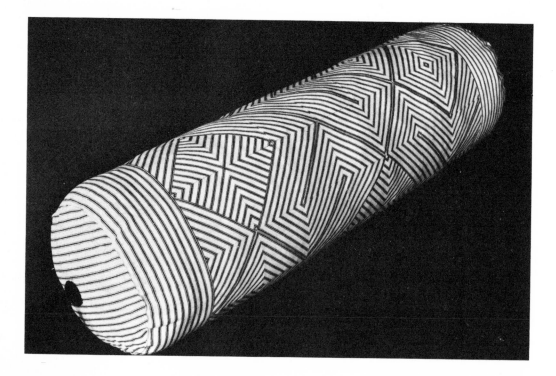

MATERIALS
Takes 1½ yards of pillow ticking or any firm fabric in regular stripes.

HOW TO MAKE
Make 56 4″ squares made up from two triangles in each of the stripe combinations shown above. Sew these together to form a patchwork fabric seven squares by eight squares. Cut two strips of fabric 4½″ wide by 32½″ long, and sew these to the 8 square sides allowing ¼″ turnings. Then either cut two circles 10″ in diameter, allowing ¼″ turnings, and sew these around both ends of bolster, leaving opening for stuffing: or preferably, make a fine cotton prototype of bolster, stuff, and then sew one circle to one end of bolster, place stuffed bolster inside, and sew remaining circle to other end. Finish with tassels at both ends.

Hexagon cushion

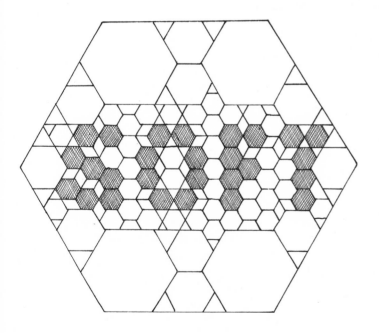

MATERIALS

Takes $\frac{1}{4}$ yard each of 5 different cotton prints. 1 yard of dark cotton print for letters spelling SOFT, and for backing. Approximately 2 lbs kapok.

By using light and dark fabrics you can work out special designs like names, initials, or even shapes of animals, houses, flowers etc.

HOW TO MAKE

Make templates for 1″ hexagons, 2″ hexagons, 1″ triangles, 2″ triangles, and 1″ diamonds. From these templates cut the following: 38 1″ hexagons; 27 1″ hexagons in dark fabric; 14 2″ triangles; 8 2″ hexagons; 2 1″ hexagons, cut in half; 30 1″ triangles; 24 1″ diamonds.

When all the pieces are cut, sew together as illustrated in diagram. Make a firm cotton prototype of cushion, and stuff with kapok. Cut backing fabric and stitch to patchwork, leaving room for stuffed cushion to go inside. Sew remaining seam of patchwork to backing.

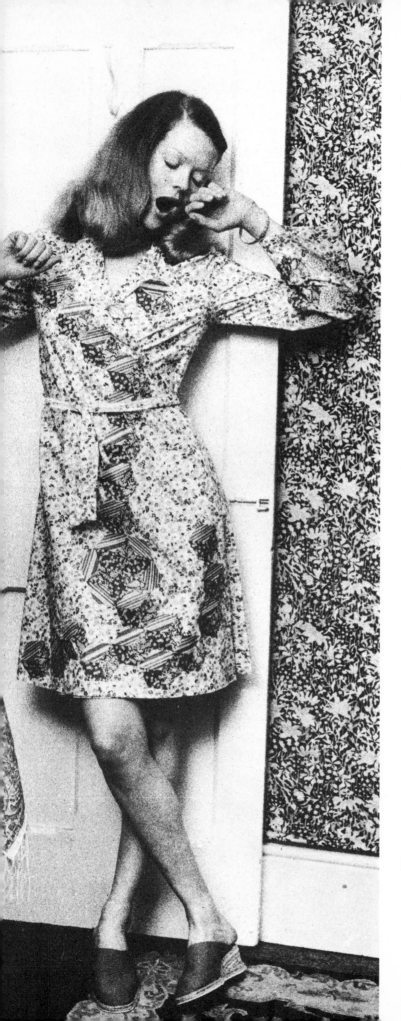

Shirtwaister dress
with appliqué patchwork

MATERIALS
Shirtwaister ~~dress pattern.~~

Size 8 takes $3\frac{1}{2}$ yards of 36″ fabric. Shown here in cotton lawn. $\frac{1}{2}$ yard each of 3 contrast cotton lawns.

HOW TO MAKE
Make dress from pattern in usual way. Then cut diamond template from illustration, and from this cut as many diamonds as desired from the three contrast lawns. Place these in a cube shape as illustrated, and sew together. When the cubes are finished, pin them in position on dress in any design you like, and either machine zig-zag or stitch to dress by hand. Cubes can also be added to the sleeves, or the single diamond shapes in bands round the sleeves will give a further pattern effect.

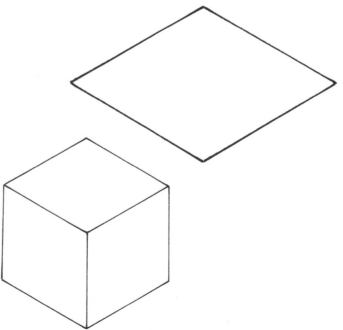

Crib cover

Designed by Janet Speak.

MATERIALS
Takes ½ yard each of 8 different fabric prints, shown here in printed lawn. 1 yard of contrast print for backing. 1 yard synthetic wadding for interlining. 4 yards lace for edging. Finished size 22″ × 29″.

HOW TO MAKE
Make the following templates: 2″ square, 2″ sided triangles, 3″ sided triangles, 2″ sided rhomboids.

From these cut: 4 2″ squares, 68 2″ sided triangles, 44 3″ sided triangles, and 26 2″ sided rhomboids.

Select your fabric for these as desired, and make up as illustrated in diagram. When patchwork is complete, stitch wadding and patchwork together (see page 50); then cut backing fabric and stitch to patchwork with lace edging sandwiched between these two layers.

This pattern can be enlarged for a big bedcover by making as many of these squares as desired.

Shell evening purse and Velvet shoulder bag

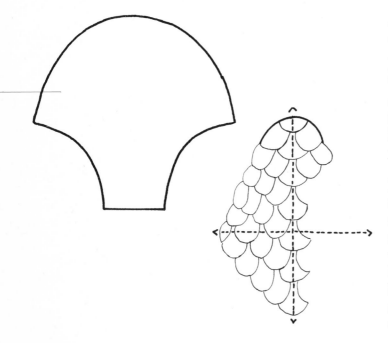

Evening purse

MATERIALS
Takes $\frac{1}{4}$ yard each of 3 shades velvet, $\frac{1}{8}$ yard of silver lamé, $\frac{1}{4}$ yard lining, and $\frac{1}{2}$ yard braid for finishing inside frame. Silver frame and handle. Frames can be found at good needlework stores or at antique shops and markets.

HOW TO MAKE
Cut template from illustration, and from it make 18 mid-tone shells, 24 light shells, 34 dark shells, and 10 lamé shells. Stitch these together in overlapping pattern as illustrated, back and front alike. Cut lining to shape of bag. Sew backs and fronts together. Fit lining, and attach frame and handle (approximately 4″ diameter semi-circle). Trim with braid.

Shoulder bag

MATERIALS
Takes $\frac{1}{2}$ yard main color dark brown velvet and $\frac{1}{4}$ yard each of two contrast color velvets, cream and tan. $\frac{1}{2}$ yard lining and interfacing. Braid to finish seams. Finished bag measures $9\frac{1}{2}″ \times 8\frac{1}{2}″$.

HOW TO MAKE
Cut template from illustration, and from it make 41 dark brown diamonds, 36 cream diamonds, and 36 tan diamonds. Make front panel as illustrated, arranging colors as photograph. Make back and flap all in one piece. Interline patchwork. Cut gusset $27\frac{1}{4}″ \times 2\frac{1}{4}″$, and interline. Cut lining to shape of bag. Join front and back panels to gusset for both bag and lining. Cut strap $2\frac{1}{4}″$ to desired length and self-line. Join strap to gusset at top edge. Fit lining and trim with braid at top edges and around flap.

Shoulder bag

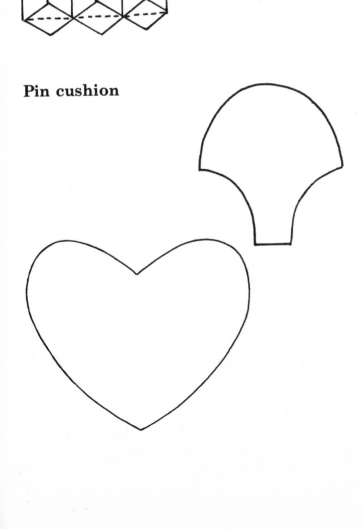

Pin cushion

Pin cushion

MATERIALS
Use small pieces of varying shades of pink, and about $\frac{1}{8}$ yard of dark pink. $\frac{1}{4}$ yard of silk for backing. Small quantity of crystal beads. Stuffing as required; upholsterer's yarn is preferable for this design. Pin cushion measures $8\frac{1}{2}'' \times 8\frac{1}{4}''$.

HOW TO MAKE
Cut template from illustration, and make 28 varying shades of pink scallops and 55 dark scallops. Cut heart shape from dark pink fabric as illustration. Sew scallops round center heart beginning with light tones, and graduating to dark. Continue until size is reached ($8\frac{1}{2}'' \times 8\frac{1}{4}''$). Cut backing to shape of heart. Cut prototype in fine cotton and stuff or sew backing to patchwork leaving opening for stuffing. Stuff, sew up, and trim with beads around edge and on patchwork as required.

Waste basket

MATERIALS
Takes $\frac{1}{2}$ yard of main color velvet, $\frac{1}{4}$ yard of second color velvet and $\frac{1}{8}$ yard each of third and fourth color velvets. Cardboard frame available from most good needlework and handicraft stores. Finished basket measures 10″ in height including 1″ bands of main fabric at top and bottom.

HOW TO MAKE
Make 2″ square template, and from this cut 48 main color squares, 24 second color squares, and 12 each of third and fourth colors. Join these diagonally in the following four-square sequence, working from top to bottom: four main color; half square, three squares and half square of second color; four main color; half square of third color, one square of fourth color, one square of third color, one square of fourth color, half square of third color; four main color; then repeat sequence until all the squares are joined together. When completed, join to make circle, and fit over frame. Cut two $2\frac{1}{2}″$ width strips long enough to fit around frame. Stitch these to patchwork at top and bottom then fold the unstitched edge inside frame and glue in position.

Letter folder

MATERIALS
Take small pieces of fabric in 10 different prints, 5 light and 5 dark; a small piece of plain fabric for centers. Finished folder is 9″ × 11″.

HOW TO MAKE
Cut a piece of thin cardboard 9″ × 11″ and using this as your template mark out center panel $2\frac{1}{4}″ × 2\frac{3}{4}″$ and strips as illustrated in photograph. Cut center panel and fabric strips from this with $\frac{1}{4}″$ seam allowance all round. Embroider center panel as required, and then starting from this join on strips of fabric remembering to do one side dark and the other pale. When first side is complete repeat exactly for second. Join both sides together. Finish edges and center panels with feather stitch. Cut piece of firm cardboard to finished size. Attach patchwork to this using clear glue, and line with paper or fabric.

Bedspread

shown on back cover

Designed by Joyce Buckingham

MATERIALS
Takes approximately 4 yards of velvet for background and border. 1 yard each of four different colored velvets. 1 yard each of four different patterned brocades – use some striped, as these form a further star shape. Lining as required for finished bedspread. Bedspread measures 6′2″ × 6′2″ approximately.

HOW TO MAKE
Make templates of 2″ hexagon and 2″ diamond. Cut 354 hexagons in various colored velvets, 42 hexagons in background velvet, 354 diamonds for centers in patterned brocades, and 184 diamonds in background velvet. Sew six brocade diamonds together in a ring to make the center, and surround this with a variety of six colored velvet hexagons for petals. This makes one unit. Make 58 more of these, and join together with diamonds of background velvet. For the best effect each center should be made in the same tones of color. When all are sewn together, cut two pieces of velvet in background color 10″ wide for length of spread plus 20″ extra on each, and two pieces 10″ wide for width of spread. Fit the short pieces between the long ones to make a square, stitch seams; then fit round patchwork section, sew, and line if required.

uilting

On the following pages we give step by step instructions on how to do quilting, both wadded quilting and Italian or cord quilting. Quilting can, of course, be used in conjunction with patchwork or as a decorated surface on plain fabric. Wadded quilting has the added attraction of being warm in use as well as beautiful. Italian or cord quilting can be used for whole areas or just as relief motifs such as initials or decorative designs.

Wadded quilting

What fabrics to choose

The choice of fabric is very important for quilting of any kind. The fabric ought to be closely woven, soft, and smooth. A washable fabric is best, since hand washing is the safest way to clean quilted work.

In deciding how much fabric to buy, it is important to remember that as much as 2″ each way may be taken up by the actual quilting in a big piece of work, and possibly at least 1″ each way on each piece of a garment. Therefore you must allow for this 'shrinkage'.

The actual wadding fabric can be traditional, such as good quality cotton batting, or a cotton wadding on a sized backing (usually sold in 12 yard lengths, 36″ wide). To make the process easier and safer when washing, you can choose a synthetic wadding which handles well and will retain its shape after a great deal of use. It is important to make sure that both the fabric and the wadding material are pre-shrunk.

Quilting can be a very real art-form. The swan on the opposite page was designed and made by artist Eirian Short

How to start

The actual stitching for quilting should be done using polyester thread (not mercerized – this is too weak) for cotton fabrics, and a strong silk thread for silk fabrics.

When you have chosen both the fabric and the wadding you are ready to start quilting. If you have chosen a traditional wadding such as cotton batting or cotton wadding, then you will need a backing fabric or cotton lining and the procedure is as follows: Lay the backing fabric on a smooth, even surface, place the wadding on top and then on top of this place the surface fabric. These three layers are then tacked together making sure that the layers are all smooth and wrinkle-free. With synthetic wadding you will not need a backing fabric; just tack on the surface fabric, but again, care must be taken to ensure that the two layers are completely wrinkle-free.

For stitching instructions see p. 50 (wadded quilting), and p. 55 (cord quilting).

Templates

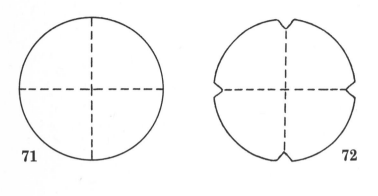

71

72

Filling stitches ('filling' means enclosing an area of fabric with stitching) such as the well-known square or diamond pattern, involve drawing straight, accurate horizontal and vertical lines; more interesting and complicated patterns can be made by the use of templates. The simplest shape to start with is the circle. Draw a circle on stiff card with a pair of compasses; cut it out. This is your template.

One circle can be moved round the fabric to make various patterns. If the circle is quartered (fig. 71), and notched at the points where the lines meet the circumference (fig. 72), this is a guide for making the circles into a border (fig. 73), a traditional wine glass pattern (fig. 74), or a shell filling pattern (fig. 75).

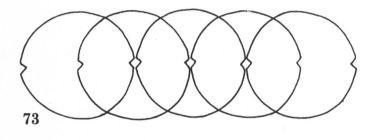

73

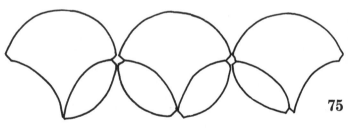

75

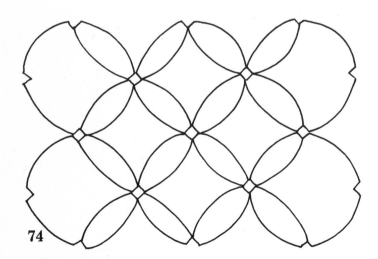

74

How to mark designs

The design is always marked on what will be the right side of the work. The important features of the design come first, working from the center to the borders.

If you are going to use templates, now is the time to decide on the size and the positioning of the design.

Having already tacked the fabric and the wadding together, begin to mark the pattern by placing a template on the fabric, and 'drawing' round it with a needle, held flat to the material, and using pressure. This makes a line-like crease (fig. 76). Inside the outline of the template, the rest of the design can be marked in the same way. If you make an error the mark can be removed by damping the material and pressing with a warm iron.

Designs can also be drawn on tracing paper, and marked through the paper onto the fabric by needle or by dressmaker's wheel and marking paper (fig. 77). Tailor's chalk can be useful for any difficult bits of pattern, it can be easily brushed off without leaving a mark. Never use an indelible pen or pencil.

It is important to remember that if you are going to work on a large area such as a bedspread where two widths of fabric are to be joined together, never have a seam down the center of the design; it is best to cut the extra fabric down the middle, and join a piece to either side of the main part (fig. 78).

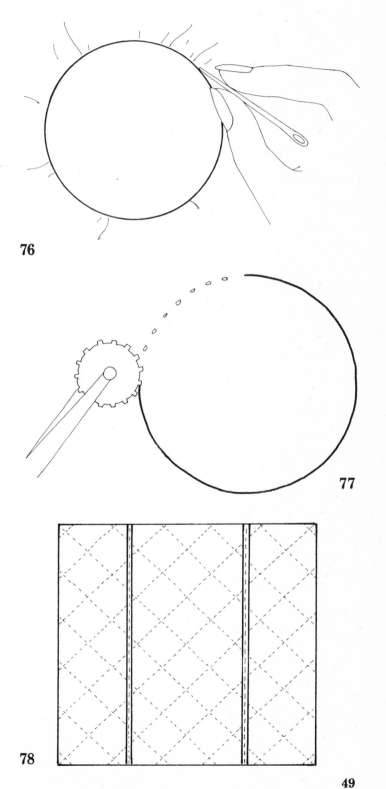

76

77

78

Quilting for garments

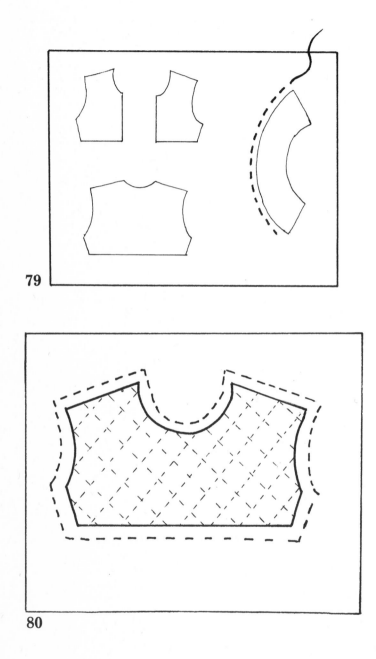

79

80

Choose which areas of the garment are to be quilted and select the pattern pieces required. Then place these pattern pieces on top of the already tacked layers of fabric and wadding. Tack all round these pattern pieces, allowing at least $\frac{1}{2}''$ all round for shrinkage (fig. 79). Quilt the pieces together using running stitch and making sure that the stitching goes through both layers of fabric. If the quilting pattern is a simple filling stitch pattern such as rectangles, diamonds or squares, then the quilting can be done by machine. When quilting has been completed, cut out the pattern pieces separately and check the final size of each piece against the original paper pattern. The quilted areas should be initially tacked together by hand, even if the rest of the garment is machined; remove the tacking stitches and make up in the usual way (fig. 80).

Patterns for wadded quilting

Traditional filling patterns are the most frequently used. The Hexagon (fig. 81) is as decorative in quilting as in patchwork and is, of course, most often used in hexagon patchwork quilts. The Shell (fig. 82) using the circular notched template is also good on its own or when used in conjunction with shell motif patchwork.

Basket weave effects using straight lines give marvelous results. You can start with a simple square pattern (fig. 83), and then with gaining confidence you can move on to a more intricate pattern (fig. 84) or a lattice pattern (fig. 85). All of these patterns look good on plain fabrics.

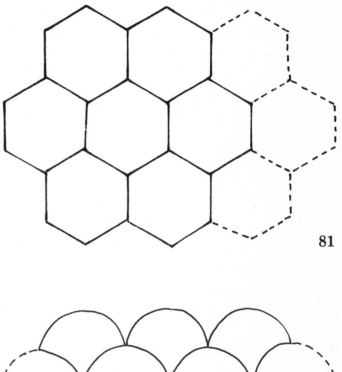

81

82

83

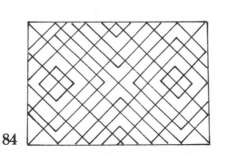

84

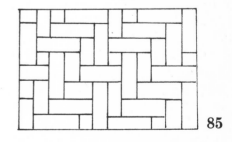

85

Traditional wadded shapes

86

87

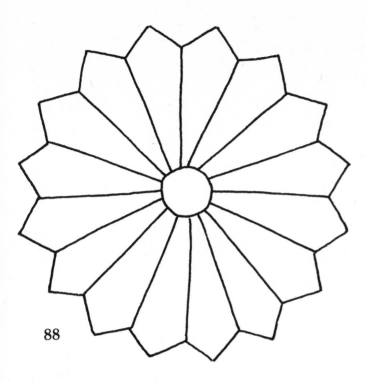

88

These four patterns can be traced from this book and used directly as a decorative motif, singly or in groups, onto any chosen design, from cushions or bedspreads or as motifs for jackets, coats etc. Fig. 86 shows the rose design; fig. 87 is the straight feather border; fig. 88 is the star, and fig. 89, the shell.

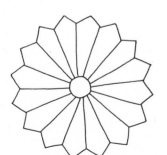

89

Italian or cord quilting

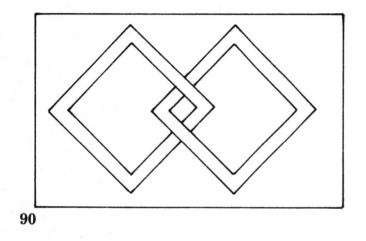

90

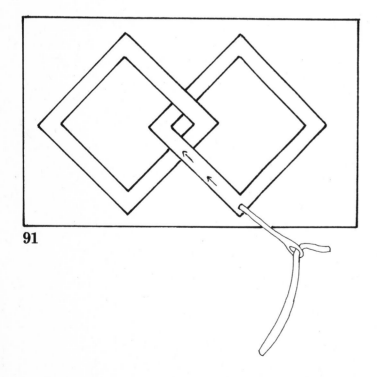

91

Cord quilting has a ridged and linear look quite different in appearance from wadded quilting. Unlike wadded quilting, which can be machined, cord quilting does have to be done by hand.

What fabrics to choose

The choice of fabric is exactly the same as for wadded quilting, except that when in doubt choose a lighter, finer fabric as opposed to a stiffer one. Light-weight closely woven fabrics achieve the best effects as the fabric will be more pliable and will 'bend' more easily when working the design.

How to start

After choosing the surface fabric, select a fine lawn or cheesecloth and on this mark out your design. Cord quilting designs are always marked on the backing fabric, not on the surface fabric. When you have marked the outline you simply add a second line inside the first to make a channel wide enough to pipe a cord through. Transfers are available from most needlecraft stores, and are specially designed for cord quilting. If you are using a transfer, then this is ironed onto the butter muslin. Lawn is best for designs marked out by a needle as described in wadded quilting, page 49.

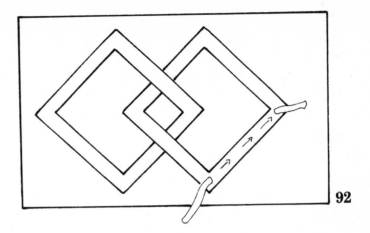

92

When the design is marked out, tack the cheesecloth or lawn to the wrong side of the surface fabric. Once more, it is important to make sure that the work is completely smooth and wrinkle-free. When all this has been done, stitch along the marked outlines with backing fabric uppermost. Running stitch is most suitable for this. When the stitching is completed (fig. 90), a cotton yarn or cord is pushed through on the wrong side (fig. 91), between the muslin and the surface fabric. This makes the ridged effect.

Use a firm cotton cord, available from good needlecraft shops in varying thicknesses, or piping cord; this, however, has to be pre-shrunk and is not always suitable for use with very fine fabric. Use a fine silk thread or buttonhole twist, and a No. 9 crewel needle for the stitching.

A bodkin is used for pushing the cord between the fabric and backing material. When using the cord do not push it round corners; to make a sharp point, the cord is pulled through the backing fabric and cut with an inch to spare (fig. 92). It can then be re-started in the new direction (fig. 93). This also applies when making an under-over pattern; the yarn or cord is brought through the backing fabric, cut and re-started (fig. 94). After cutting the one inch ends leave them exactly as they are, they will not move.

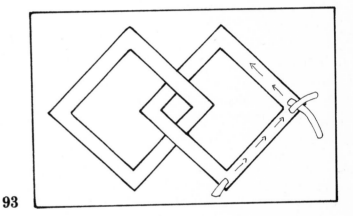

93

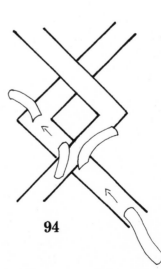

94

Cord quilting patterns

95

96

The templates used for wadded quilting can also be used for Italian or Cord quilting, but two parallel lines of stitching must be made. Fig. 95 shows the hexagon, fig. 96 illustrates the shell.

The chevron effect is useful for borders such as around a bedspread or the hem of a skirt (fig. 97).

An entire surface can be covered with an interlaced pattern (fig. 98).

A circular template used for interlocking circles gives a very decorative edging (fig. 99).

Edging and corner patterns

The following patterns can be used for either wadded or cord quilting. These designs can be used direct by marking out the individual motifs given beside the big designs. Figs. 100 and 100a show eighteenth century wave edging, circular wave border is shown in 101 and 101a, and in figs. 102 and 102a are the double hammock edging showing the template and its placing for the design.

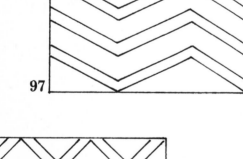

97

98

99

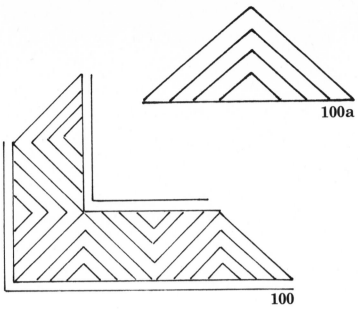

100a

100

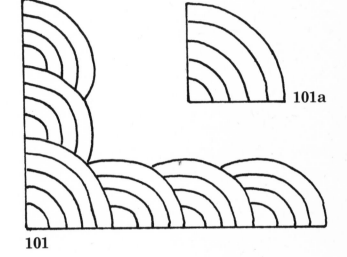

101a

101

102a

102

57

Edging and corner patterns

Fig. 103 shows twist edging with its template, and fig. 103a shows how to align it. It gives a beautiful rope effect (fig. 103b). Though this particular design is more suitable for wadded quilting, it can also be adapted for cord quilting simply by adding a second row of stitching to make a channel the width of the cord to be used, inside the given outline.

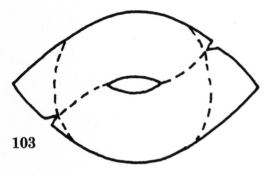

103

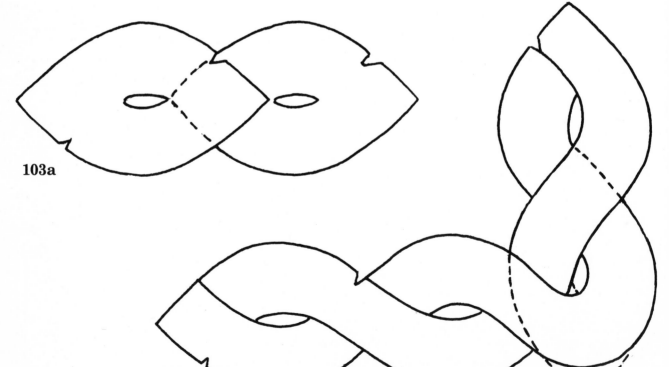

103a

103b

Finishing

Quilted designs can be finished in several ways:

The edges can be turned in and stitched together, then a second row of stitching close to the first row is added to keep it firm (fig. 104).

Turn the edges in, then insert a piping cord which has been covered with bias strips of the main fabric. Stitch this between the two edges (fig. 105).

Bind the edges with bias cut strips of the main fabric (fig. 106).

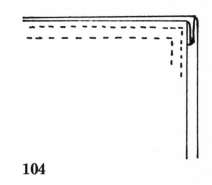

104

Washing and care

Patchwork
Provided care has been taken in the original selection of the fabrics and the color tested for fastness before use, you should be able to wash your patchwork by hand, using mild soap flakes and hand-hot water. Patchwork must be dried flat and pressed with care, to prevent 'bagging'.

If there is any doubt about the original choice of fabric then the patchwork should be dry-cleaned.

Quilting
Quilts padded with cotton batting or felt ought to be dry-cleaned to prevent the wadding shrinking. Quilts made with synthetic fibres and wadding can be washed carefully by hand and dried flat. All quilts should be cleaned or washed before they get really dirty. When washing never rub or wring, but handle gently.

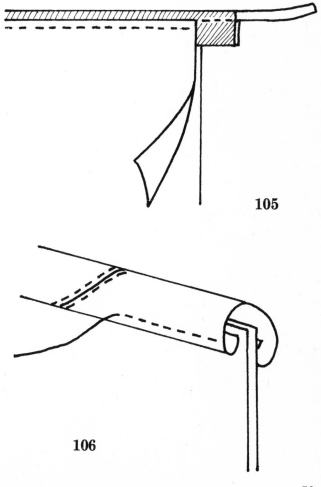

105

106

Bedjacket

MATERIALS

Straight short jacket pattern which can translate into an evening jacket by using a darker satin and omitting the swansdown trimming.

Size 8 takes 2 yards 36″ satin, 2 yards wadding, 2 yards swansdown trimming, and 2 yards lining. The yoke and sleeves are rectangle quilting and the rectangles measure $1\frac{3}{4}″ \times \frac{3}{4}″$.

HOW TO MAKE

A Fleur de lys style template (fig. A) is used for the bodice. Cut template from fig. A, and then mark up on fabric as given (fig. B).

Make up quilting as given on page 50 and when completed, make up garment in the usual way.

B

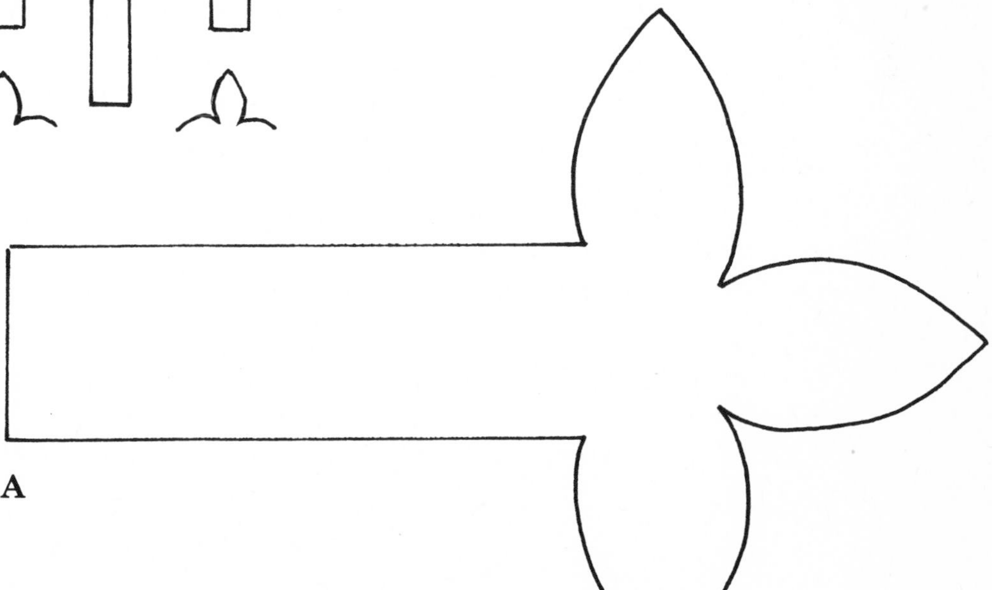

A

Flannel jacket

MATERIALS

Classic jacket with all-in-one yoke and sleeves. Padded with Terylene.

Size 8 takes 2⅛ yards of 45″ fabric, 2½ yards 36″ lining, and 3 yards of Terylene wadding.

HOW TO MAKE

The quilting is 1″ squares using twin needles on machine to give pin tuck effect. This could also be done by hand using two channels of stitching close together. Daisy design is used for yoke and corners (see below).

Print jacket

MATERIALS

Very easy to make loose fitting jacket with tie belt.

Size 8 takes 3 yards cotton in main color, and 1 yard contrast.

HOW TO MAKE

The jacket is quilted all over in 1⅞″ squares. First make up the quilting (see p. 50 for instructions), then make up the garment according to the instructions with the pattern.

Italian or cord quilt over-blouse

Quilting designed by Susan Duckworth

MATERIALS
Loose fitting, yoked over-blouse with full sleeves.

Size 8 takes $3\frac{1}{4}$ yards 36″ fabric, 1 yard fine muslin or cheesecloth for backing, 5 buttons. Unspun soft fleece for cording available at most needlecraft stores.

HOW TO MAKE
Trace out pattern given on following pages and mark onto muslin. Then place together with surface fabric as given on page 58, and stitch channels. Pipe through four thickness of fleece cord to give high relief. When cording is finished, make up pattern in usual way.

This is a difficult pattern with some very intricate motifs. The simplest motif to use is shown in fig. A, and the design will be effective if just used on its own and repeated down the fronts of over-blouse in any desired grouping. All these motifs can be used for other purposes such as cushions, mats, and even bedspreads.

A

Ancient and modern quilting and patchwork

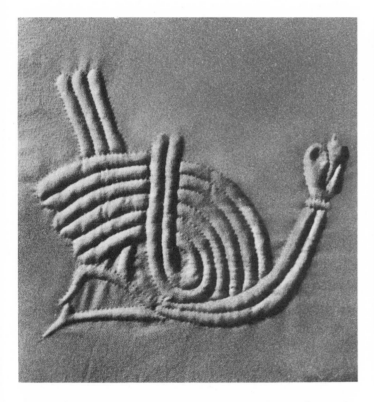 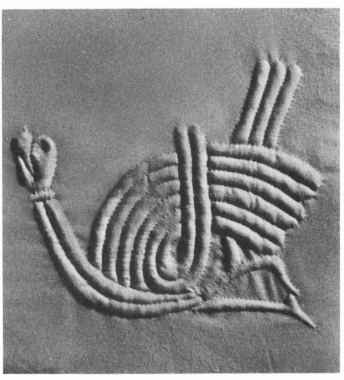

Bird design by Susan Duckworth and made in cord quilting. This motif could be made larger or smaller and used as a central motif

alone or as a bordering using a flight of smaller birds

The Blue House designed and made by Patricia Hopcraft and exhibited at the Revival of Art in Needlework Exhibition. Miss Hopcraft uses both wadded and cord quilting in this picture together with a profusion of embroidery for the garden

The State Bed of Erthig on loan to the Victoria & Albert Museum from Mr Philip Yorke dates back to 1720 and was the culminating work of art in a series of state rooms. The coverlet is made of chinese hand embroidered satin stitched in back stitch to form a quilted twisted rope pattern. Embroidered peacocks are applied to each corner of the coverlet and blend with the coloring of the headboard and curtains

Linen coverlet made by N Ward and dated 1680. Embroidered in yellow silk, the quilt stitches used in the overlapping arches include wineglass, shell, diamond filling, and line filling patterns. The central border is stitched in rope pattern. This is a superb example of quilt stitches used on their own to achieve a subtle but very beautiful textured design

Rich silk embroidery is offset with shell pattern for this early 18th century cushion cover. The fabric is satin and the background shell quilt pattern worked in back stitch of gold thread makes a rare and beautiful object

Mid-19th Century American patchwork using strips and squares. This work is known as pineapple and log cabin work and the effect can be extremely beautiful when the fabrics are carefully chosen to both blend and contrast

Mid-19th century English patchwork using running feather, shell, rosette, and flower patches. It is interesting to know that both the shell and feather patterns were originally taken from quilting designs

English patchwork circa 1805. This amazing work tells stories of domestic and military life in little scenes around the border while the central circle depicts George III at a Volunteer Review in 1803. The patchwork background is made of circles and filling patches. The circles themselves are divided in a variety of ways. Around the central picture the face of the sun is embroidered on three of the circles

Silk Patchwork Quilt made in 1835 by Emma Jane Townsend as a wedding gift for her neice Anne Overend Ramsbothom. The gift and marriage are commemorated in two beadwork circles on the quilt. One reads 'For AOR with love' and the other 'from EJT 1833'. Many of the circular motifs are delicately embroidered in silk, beads, or fish scale sequins. Some of the silver gauze used in the work is said to come from the wedding dress of Queen Charlotte. The circular motif in the middle leads into dart shapes which in turn are capped with hearts in two colors. The gate patterning round the center and border is also patchwork. Photographed by kind permission of Blaise Castle House Museum, Henbury, Bristol, where the quilt is housed

77

Patchwork does not have to be very complicated to achieve the best results. These two photographs show some recent patchworks made and designed by Mrs Derrick Amoore, who uses these hexagon shapes for room length curtains with a plain background, in multicolors for lampshades, and blending colors for cushions. The bedspread is feather stitched, and in places some of the plain patches are embroidered with flowers or small pictures

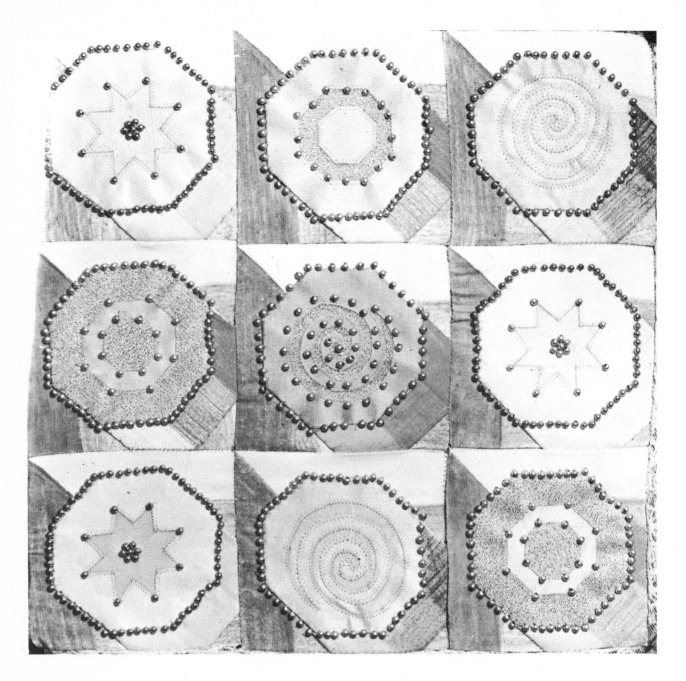

'Box of Sweets' designed and made by Eirian Short. Life-like sweets in pastel colors and decorated with beads become a witty and pretty wall-hanging.